Kruser's Point of View

By Alec Gould

Alec Gould, author of the following books:

- **We Really Need To Laugh**

All rights reserved. Copyright under Berne Copyright Convention, Universal Copyright Convention, and Pan-American Copyright Convention. No part of this book may be reproduced, stored in a retrieval system, or transmitted in any form, or by any means, electronic, mechanical, photocopying, recording or otherwise, without prior permission of the author.

A   Jumping   Cat   Publication

www.AlecGould.com
© 2018 by Alec Gould

Kruser's Point of View

Welcome...................................... 9

We Begin… 13

It's All about the Ride, ... 23

Not What You Ride 23

Beverage and a Burger........... 31

Hibernation.............................. 43

Biker Community 51

A Perked Pot o' Coffee........... 59

I'm Backkkkkkkk! 69

We Just Are… 77

Campin', Kruser-Style............ 89

You Just Might Find… 97

Hurry Up and Wait?............. 105

Frozen Thoughts 111

Baby Moons and Memories. 119

Hal's, Bikes and Bears…Oh My! 127

Now's the Time to Think Outside the Box 135

War 145

Black and White 155

My Brother's Keeper?........... 167

IMAGES 175

Sprocket Connection 185

Ancestral Ride 191

Thank you! 207

Lady G and Her Big "O" 211

Halle and Me 221

Final Thoughts 231

Welcome

This book consists of every column I had written for "Kruser's Point of View" for the two years the magazine was in production.

With that said, please keep in mind, there will be some repetition in some of the endings as these are taken word-for-word the way they were written for my column.

I have a "unique" way of writing; or so I have been told.

In this book, you shall see that these "stories" are not your usual "biker stories". Sure, there is some drinking and riding –of course riding, but more than that, they are "off the cuff".

In some cases, they are "what is happening at the time" stories or just my crazy thoughts going thru my head that happen to end up written down here.

Why is that? Oh, hell, anyone can write the usual stories, so this is where I come in, for something a wee bit different.

These stories will get you possibly talking at the drinking hole, round the camp fire or any other place you may need a "conversation starter". (That's

CONVERSATION starter, NOT fire starter. ☺)

Enjoy my friends and, as always, keep it safe! I'd like to meet you on the road someday…

~Kruser

We Begin…

As I sit here at the keyboard letting the words come thru my fingertips, B.B. King is playing in the background, a Pernat Haase brat sits in waiting to be devoured and it's finally raining a wee bit. You would think life was great.

Well, there are those times where, hell, it isn't. We've all been there. The worse part, we'll all have those days again….just different reasons, different stresses, or maybe the same ones.

That's life and it sucks.

Now, what can we do to make those "stresses" in life seem just a wee bit better than they appear to us?

Well, we can drink our favorite…or non-favorite… beverage until we pass out and wake up with a hang-over that, at my age, can last for days.

Or, depending upon what the "stress" may be, we could spout off on Facebook thinking our Facebook "friends" will help us thru it and set us straight.

(Personally, I owe a sincere apology to all my Facebook "friends" - and those involved - for using this tactic to de-stress myself.
It was idiotic and immature and I apologize).

OK, now that we've tried those two things sit down and ask yourself: "What do I really enjoy that will get me away from this stress without hurting myself or those around me?"

Think…think….think……HEY,
I
LOVE
BIKING!!!!!!!!!

Yes……….I……….do.

But is it going to help the situation/stress in my life? Well, nothing else is helping so what do I have to lose? Maybe I can get out in the wind, lose some more of my hair to Mother Nature's breath and stop to smell the roses? Ok, so I took an overnight run to the ABATE campgrounds up in the Greenwood area.

Well, this is nice...just a couple of tents in one little area set up in an Indian-style camp formation. Except the

tents weren't tee pees, there were iron horses instead of Painted horses and the wagon that was there wasn't a Pioneers' buck board but a Suburban. Still, not many people around. Great! I can get some "me time" to "clean my mind out".

Little did I know a few short hours

later the whole band of bikers and myself would be "enjoying the night" by talking, tossing the "bull" and polishing off a gallon of homemade wine, a bottle of 2-fingers Tequila and too many beers to count.

Yuppers, all 6 of us partied like it was 1980. Yes, 1980….because that song "Forever Young" comes to play after the first 1/2s gallon of wine and Tequila mixed with beer goes down…

Well, that was a good time. Now, stumble to the tent and get some shut eye.

Morning comes way too early.

After admitting to myself this tent has now become a sauna, I crawl out and meet the sun. Like coming out of the womb, my eyes ache in the brightness of Sol as I make my entry into the world.

Today brings the departure of my newly made friends and a day of solitude for me.

Much needed solitude, for as much fun and priceless as the previous night was, I still need to gather my thoughts.

After a morning of visiting with my new amigos, they leave me with a plate of cheese, sausage and crackers so as I may not starve. (Apparently, they really thought I am pregnant). So, I graciously accept their offer of food and wave "til later" as they contact their rubber orbs to the gravel road that will take them home by day's end.

I turn around, face my tent some hundred yards away and … refill my water bottle.

Damn good tequila and wine though. *burp*

I take the day to sit, get my thoughts organized and make a mental list of positives and negatives.

I took a walk around the whole perimeter of the campgrounds.

I picked up some garbage that had gotten away from the confines of their doom. Then something in the rafters caught my eye. I wonder who this Panty Pigeon belongs to?

I got A LOT more water….and I thunk. Yuppers just like Winnie the Pooh. I thunked and I thunked and I thunked.

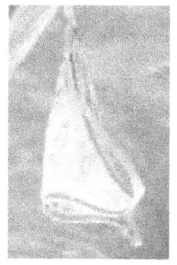

After quite a few hours of this, well, I couldn't thunk no more, no more. But, I was able to get my mind to a greater plateau than it had been before I arrived upon my iron horse a sunrise before. (OK, a GOODER plateau).

I packed up my iron steed, turned the key to Paradise on and began the trip back to my home20. On the way, I stopped to smell the roses. Granted, they aren't always roses but an old truck on the side of the black  ribbon is pretty close to a rose for this old man.

I enjoyed the scenery beneath the darkening clouds and came home refreshed and a wee bit better of a human being.

Now, 'tis true that this article wasn't all about riding nor was it about anything except "clearing your mind". But you know what? A bike got me to that greater plateau of inner peace.

Keep in mind, there's a reason you never see a bike parked outside a psychiatrist's office. Now, get out there, keep it safe and "clear your mind".

Oh, I believe it's time to eat… come here my little Pernat Haase brat. Mmmmm

P.S.: Just as I finished this article, I took a tick out of my head. Unbelievable! Yet, the great north beckons me to return soon and, I've got the key to Paradise.

It's All about the Ride, Not What You Ride

So, the other day a guy I know stops over at my place to shoot the bull for a bit. Not a close friend, not a stranger, just a guy I see every now and then.

He's a decent person. His girlfriend is nice and down to Earth and he has a brood of sensible kids. Bottom line, he's a nice person.

So, where is this going???

Well, up until about the time he turned 44, he was riding a crotch rocket. Not only that, but his girlfriend rode with him. Yuppers, they'd don themselves in all the wrong riding gear: sandals, shorts…..if they would've rode in a circle one could've sworn you were watching two orangutans doing it on a bike at the circus. It was NOT a good site to see.

Still, a nice couple when one gets past that vision.

Onto the visit from, oh let's call him…Spike?

So, Spike comes over and begins to talk about a "riding" vacation he had taken with his new (noncrotch-rocket) bike, a Yamaha.

Spike stated he had put on a few thousand miles in a week and a half.

Really "burned" the pavement, getting the wind in what little hair he has left…..and enjoying being out and away from the everyday responsibilities we all face.

During this trip, Spike had made a few stops at some Harley dealerships. At one, he was asked why he was riding a piece of "crap". At another his bike was spit upon. (None of these issues we're done by any of the dealership's personnel but by "bikers" on the premises).

Spike's response, "hey, at least I'm riding a bike. Isn't that what matters?"

Now, follow the bullet points:

- Should this have happened? NO!
- Does it really matter what we all ride? NO!
- Does it matter what we wear, where we go, who we are? NOOOOO!
- Do I like crotch rockets? NO!
- Do I believe in riding in shorts and sandals? Hell NO!
- Do I care for fellow bikers that don't wave back? No. (Yet I can understand why some don't. Either safety or….they can't find the darn "wave back button").
- Is fuchsia really a word much less a color???
  Hmmmm

Sorry, got on a roll. (Damn ADD) Now, back to the
main reason for this article…

The bottom line is correct in what Spike had stated. The only thing that does matter is THAT HE RIDES! Remember people, the more riders we have out here on the black ribbon the better off we will be down the line when "big brother" wants to limit -or ban us- from our freedoms.

Yes, we all have issues with one another. That is just the human way. Hey, my way of thinking, or riding, or whatever is better than the next guy/gal.
Ahhhhh…bull.

Your way and my way -and our brothers/sisters ways- of riding are good for that individual doing the riding.

Is there a better, safer way we could all benefit from in our riding habits? I'm sure there are, but that is not the intent of this article.

The intent is to remind us all that we aren't better than anyone else, no matter what we may think because of whom we are or what we ride.

When I began riding in 1984 I had very little money. This meant, in order for me to get a bike, I had to give up some of life's pleasures. Man was I dehydrated that year!

Eventually, I bought a 1984 Honda Night Hawk then traded that in on a 1984 Naked Wing.
Why a Wing and not a Harley?

Because I thought I couldn't afford a Harley Davidson "cool bike".

What do I have in my garage now? I have a 1981 Honda 175, 1983 Suzuki 550 and a 2004 Sportster. This past spring I had sold my 1983 Aspencade.

Does having a Honda or a Suzuki make me any less a biker than if I only owned the Sportster? No. Being a biker is in my blood, not in the make and model of the bike I ride.

So, in conclusion, no matter what we ride…..I'm cool, you're cool, we're all cool.

Let's respect one another.

Now, I shall let the words of the great philosopher, Red Green, echo in your ears til next month: "We're all in this together".

Hey, I think it's a Smurfy day for a ride. Be safe my friends!

Beverage and a Burger

Well, winter is almost officially here now, according to the calendar. According to my love, Lady G, winter IS here.

You see, Thanksgiving Day -after we watched the Macy's parade and the dog show on TV- Lady G and I hopped on the old iron horse and went for a ride. Lady G enjoyed the ride just as much as I did; the weather being great for that time of year.

Dec. 2, the weather is still great for this time of year, but what I heard out of Lady G was not, "Oh, good, we can go for a ride today!" Instead, Lady G's reply was, "Have fun".

Now, Lady G did tell me to be safe. Definitely biker smart she is, as she also told me to keep an extra eye open for the cages. Why? Because they wouldn't be as used to seeing a bike out on the road as they had been this past summer.

So, what did I do when I heard I was going for a solo ride? Well, I went straight downstairs and got my leathers. A few minutes later, I reappeared in chaps, battery operated hunting socks and raccoon hat. Oh ya, jacket and gloves too.

Hey, you take the wind chill factor of 45 degrees into consideration and you get what I call…c-c-cold! But still, a great day to go for a ride!

Now, I had thought about getting gas before leaving town, but upon checking the trip meter, I had enough to put a few miles on the old steed right at the get-go. I mean, hey, it's been awhile since I had taken Paradise out for a ride and I thought it best to get her out before she got all wild and began to act like she was in some rodeo…and I didn't feel like being the clown she was going to "buck off".

Well, I opened the gates of the corral and off we went, Paradise and myself, into the afternoon sun. Wait, there was NO sun. Actually, it was all clouds. Either way, we left the corral and headed down the trail towards Portage.

Why Portage? Best burger place -in my book- in the length of miles I thought I could get in this aft.

You see, I thought I might follow 33 towards the setting sun until I got to 73 North. Then hook up to F to Portage. After my burger and "re-hydration beverage", I had pondered taking "P" South towards Cambria and The Dump, then homewards bound via "P" and 33 East.

As you'll read, that is, if you finish this article, you'll see I never did take that "plan of action". Then again, some of the best times are those that are unplanned.

Well, pulling into the gas station to feed Paradise, I could tell it was getting closer to Christmas time. Yuppers, Elvis (NOT ELVES), but Elvis himself was singing "Santa Claus is Coming to Town" over the speakers.

Pulling up to a "feeder", I was a bit surprised at the amount of boats that were behind the cages, as I thought they would've been stored some time ago. Then again, I believe some people thought that I was the crazy one, being out on the bike and all. One mother even "coached" her young son away from my "feeder area" and told him to follow her as she glared in my direction, uneasy like. (It must've been my raccoon hat that set her off.)

Well, after taking my receipt for Paradise's feed, I got back out onto the trail…I mean road.

As Paradise gained momentum, the sun teased us for a few seconds to show us it could come out…if it wanted to…but it didn't want to, as it then went back behind the clouds.

I began to think how the cowboys did it with real live, blood driven horses. How they battled the cold and were unable to put on as many miles that I will have by sun's end.

The sights of Christmas decorations and the smell of wood burning to keep some of the country homes warm, well; it was a beautiful day for a ride. Not a single bike out except myself. Was it because of the cold or because the Packers were preparing to beat the Vikings?

Coming into Portage, I spied off to the side of the road, three men swinging their woods at the golf course. Rounding the corner in town, I spied a man in a Packer jersey and another man wearing Viking "horns". See, winter is NOT here…football season is.

My thoughts turned towards the guy with the Viking horns; seemed a bit out of place in Packer land. That's when I remembered I was wearing a raccoon hat riding a motorcycle in Dec. Yup; the guy with the Viking horns WAS out of place.

A few blocks down, I pulled upon the reins of Paradise and tied her up in the lot at Lane's Full Throttle. Best place for burgers in the area! Yet, there was only one other bike there.

Go figure!

Upon my entry, I noticed most of the patrons were down at the far end of the bar. Yes, the Packers were on TV. Oh, and so were the Vikings.

I ordered up a beverage and a burger with the works via Sheryl, the bartender; then began my warm up process.

Yes, that is better. Hydration is very important no matter what the season!

Well, the talk in the bar was basically on the football game; yet on the end I was at, the conversation turned toward riding the Mississippi route. The couple near me owns a place along the route and they were telling me about the back roads and local scenery that many aren't aware of by simply riding thru.

Now, Lady G and I had ridden the route from La Crosse down to Wyalusing Park this past summer. We had taken the big road until we got to

Lacrosse and Buzzard Billy's, then it was 35 South. It was a beautiful ride to say the least.

Yet, talking with Ron and Kari, they could show Lady G and me a lot more than we could find on our own. Yes; back roads with great views is a biker's paradise. (Hey, that's the name of my bike!)

Well, the hours slipped by, the Packers were on their way to another win, and I had made three new friends.
I happened to look up at the hands on the wall and they stated it was near three pm.

Time to saddle up and mosey on home to Lady G before Sol calls it a day.

I shake a few hands, collect a phone number and bid my new friends goodbye.

As I get Paradise pointed homeward bound, I recall the roads I was going to take that afternoon.
Nopers, not half of those roads would be seen this day.

Yet, the road took me to new friends, friends I will meet again someday.

We will ride together on the back roads of the mighty Mississippi and other destinations unknown at this time. Who knows; maybe new roads to new friendships together?

It's not always the destination that's the pinnacle of the ride. Sometimes it's the ride itself. Sometimes it's the people and places you see. Sometimes, maybe sometimes, it's the friends you make along the way.

Until next month my friends….stay safe, stay warm.

Hibernation

I've had it!

Yes, the winter hasn't been all too bad upon us in my area…'cept the 20½ inches of snow we got that one day and the 7½ inches of snow we got yesterday with the minus temps. Other than that, it's been…crappy.

I'm not going to pussy foot around it, it is winter.

Yuck!

Granted, I could move south but I do like the north woods to visit and the

Horicon Marsh to hunt and photograph. The Kettle Moraine to ride in; and also to see the big parade in Eagle the last Sunday of June…my home town. The south west area for rides and the east coast of the state to meander along Lake Michigan. Let us not forget the great Mississippi River Road and its included areas such as the bluffs, coulees, etc.

So, I guess you could say I am well centered. Not well balanced, but well centered in this fine state of Wisconsin.

Still, winter for a biker is always too long of a season. I mean, hey, we only need a day to get our bikes ready to ride again. That is, if we have everything organized and at the ready.

Fortunately, I did get some riding in thru the first half of December but then the snows hit. It was a terrible blizzard. 20½ inches of snow fell in 24 hours. I couldn't see in front of me, the wind was blowing all around. I did not know what to do. Gifts that were wrapped were rolling down the streets; Elves were clinging onto whatever they could to keep from being whisked away. It was horrible! Then, all of a sudden, Rudolph with his nose so bright gave me an idea….HOLD IT!!!! Geez Kruser; put the JD down….. I'm a sorry folks…that was another "story". Now, where was I?

Brrrrrr. I have made it thru January.

Now, it's February and Paradise is still waiting to roll her rubbers out onto the  black ribbon of "life as we know it".

I must say, for a short month, Lady G and I are going to be very busy as we hope you are also. You see, with February comes a beckoning from many places to get our cabin-fevered selves out and about.

We've got an event for Dave Sky in a few weeks. He's a great guy in many different areas that I'm afraid most people don't know. He plays Santa in his spare time all the way to playing music where-ever he can. As a matter of fact, most of you might know Dave from going to the Loon Party held in Mercer, WI. He's always there playing some great music and get this, when he's not playing he's helping out with the Loon Party in any way he can. Yes indeed, a heart of gold that man has.

We also have a "Chili Feed" put on by the Sleep Watchers M.C. on another Saturday. They are a great group of people. S.W.M.C. will be giving a portion of the proceeds to the Dells Area Food Pantry.

At the end of the month we hope to be able to go to the Jefferson Swap meet and get together with my bro, David aka "Digger", and his wife Beth.

Yes, a few of many things to be going to in which it will be nice to see faces we haven't seen in some time. Face Book keeps a lot of us in contact, but there is nothing like a good old biker hug and a "gripping" handshake to keep the bond solid.

Well, when we aren't traveling in the cage, we will be going thru pamphlets, maps and web sites to get our inner beings peaked for possible trips this year. That and looking thru photos of last year, just to keep our hearts warm and beating for a new year of riding.

So, I hope Ol' Man Winter loosens his grip on all of us, Jack Frost lets our noses alone and the Wicked Witch of the Winter North stops breathing her chill down our backs.

Until the spring rains remove the seasoning of this past winter from its roads, Paradise is still in her stall waiting to get out. Me? I'm enjoying hibernation the best I can, with Lady G wrapped up in my arms.

Til next month my friends, stay warm and stay safe.

~Kruser

Biker Community

Well, my biker brothers and sisters, as I begin this article it is cold outside.

Christmas and New Years are past, and I long to go riding.

Yet, 20 ½ inches of snow in one day put a damper on that for me and Paradise. That was a week ago, now the salt trucks are basting the roads….

I did get my 2013 budget made and - still- never enough money. Yet, Lady G and I shall be going on as many bike trips as possible, so long as time allows and gas is in the tank.

We are thinking of possibly doing the Ohio H.O.G. run this year, along with a trip or two to upper Michigan. Yes, there will be a few trips to the North woods of Wisconsin.

We hope to get back over to the "Save the Tatas" poker run over in Avoca, as we had been there two years ago, and it was a great event, great ride, and of course, great people.

We may also do a ride or two with the Patriot Guard Riders in honor of those who serve and have served.

Who knows, maybe we will get to Sturgis this year?

The plans are on the board.

Yet, as nice as most of those rides are for us, it is those rides in which we participate to help our fellow bikers that really bring us together. Because, one thing for sure is, if we are needed, we are there for each other.

If one of us goes down, the rest of us will be there to help. Could be to mow their lawn, take their kids to school or to have a money-making event to help them with living and medical expenses.

It doesn't matter to us if we know them personally or see an article in a biker rag.

Heck, it may only be a "holler" across the bar if we need a ride home or help in finding where our tent is located…again.

At the drop of a: wet t-shirt, feather, drip of oil – whatever word you'd like to use….we will be there to help when we can.

Then, there are those times we hear of events in which we can't do anything.

Times in the not so long ago past: jets going into sky scrapers, bombs blowing up buildings, soldiers and civilians whom have lost their lives; our kids and teachers shot and killed.

Just as we all bleed red; our hearts also break; biker "tough" or not. No doubt, it affects us all.

Then, you know what happens? We pick ourselves up by the boot straps and ask, "What can we do to ease the pain and make things a wee bit better for those who need us?"

We may not be able to reverse time, but we can at least make the hurt, hurt a little less. Be it for a cancer run or a memorial ride.

Unless you are -or were- a member of the Armed Forces or of the police, fire and rescue departments, the last time many of us may have been part of such a group would have been high school. Years ago my neighbors would wonder if I was a "good neighbor".

"Look out for that man and his leather clad girlfriend", they would say. "I don't know about those two. Better lock your kids up and keep the dog in, they don't look safe…"

Now that they know me and Lady G, they have let the kids and dog back outside.

We wear leathers, our hair may be long, and we have tattoos. We are a "Biker Community" and I am damn proud to be a member.

Till next month my friends, stay warm, stay healthy….and stay safe!

A Perked Pot o' Coffee

RRRRRRR, I do NOT do mornings well!

Birds have their wings pulled over snoring beaks, worms are cuddled in

Mother Earth's womb, Sol is stretching, attempting to get himself raised, and Alec-the-Cat is looking at me like, "Hey, it's not time to feed me yet! Lie back down and rub my ears".

Meanwhile, Lady G is zonked out to a land of peacefulness, no stress, and lots of sunshine. What the heck am I doing awake?

Well, I am, so I might as well get up and get the day started.

Alec-the-Cat jumps off the bed to hurry me into "feed the cat" mode and multi-tasked that into a toothy yawn.
As for myself, I'm trying to do the best I can at dressing myself in the all-too-early morning hours.

Oh…my…gosh! It's only 7am!!!

Since I'm already at this stage in the morning ritual, I figure I might as well finish getting dressed and get Alec-the-Cat her food before I end up with one teed off…feline.

With Alec fed, and my morning ritual done: teeth brushed, toilet flushed, the usual task, that's when it dawns on me: It's SATURDAY!

This is great! Here I thought it was Friday. Well, this isn't too bad now. Since I've gotten up early –yes, EARLY- the day is only going to get better.

In anticipation of Lady G getting up soon, I head for the kitchen to perk a pot o' coffee and toast some bread.

A wee bit later, Alec comes in licking her lips, showing me she has once again approved of my taking care of her which means I get to live another day. Hooray!

The coffee begins to "perk-perk-perk" and Lady G enters the kitchen with a faint smile. A peck on the cheek and she heads off to brighten her toothies and get herself ready to start the day.

I proceed to pour some go-go juice into my coffee cup and then oblige Lady G of the same; placing hers on the table for her arrival.

Locating myself at the table, I chomp on the toast and wait for My Love to return so we may discuss our day to be.

We enjoy these times; sipping on a cup of perked coffee and talking about anything that may come to our attention to share with each other.

As Lady G seats herself across the table from me, I ask her if she would like to take a ride to Eagle's Nest up in Princeton. Lady G jumps at the chance to go for a ride with a jubilant "YES!"

Perfect, our day is set with a great ride on Hwy 73. Along with that, we will have a nice visit with Angie, the owner, and a delicious perch dinner.

I feel the brush on my leg as Alec joins the two of us

Lady G and I talk; every now and then Alec breaking our words with a "meow".

I pour myself a second cup of go-go juice from the perk-pot and a half cup for Lady G as we decide where else we can go on our ride.
A short time later, we have our plans and route determined. We know that we won't stick with it, but it gives us a starting point. Princeton.

Lady G states that she'll turn the coffee pot off and take care of the few dishes if I wish to get Paradise ready. No need for a reply, I head for the stable.

Going out to the stall I release Paradise out onto the drive, check her oil, and clean the windshield, lights and mirrors. (Last night we returned too late to do the cleanings).

I await Lady G's arrival which comes quick. She comes towards me with a big smile on her face as Paradise releases a mighty roar.

As Lady G gets up in the saddle, she wraps her arms around me, presses against my back and whispers in my ear, "Honey".

I smile and wait for her to continue.

"Honey", she says again as she presses into my back with her chest.

I begin to smile, a BIG smile.

"Honey, it's time to get up. Remember, we had a lot of snow during the night and you need to clean the sidewalks and the driveway so I can get to the store".

The smile dissipates, my eyes slowly open; I become aware of where I am.

"Honey, can you get up now?" she asks me again.

"Yes, My Love. I'll get up."

I proceed to roll over and pull the blankets over my head.

I finish my reply: "when it's spring."

'til next month my friends; keep it safe and get your steeds ready. Riding season IS around the corner.

I'm Backkkkkkkk!

Good evening my Brothers and Sisters of the Covenant of the Black Ribbon! Yes, I know, it has been awhile, my apologies.

This "old" body of mine decided to give me some issues and, well, let's just say I'm doing a wee bit better now. This, in a sideways effect, is a wee bit sad. Why? Well, those damn pain pills were outstanding! I...could...FLY!

Problem was Lady G and I was not able to get on the bike with those in my system. Suffice it to say, I've been off the pain meds for a while now and we are getting Paradise some much needed exercise.

During this "off time" I've been keeping busy repairing/restoring old photos, a nice sit down job. I also showed my support for the Michigan families at the court procedure in Fond du Lac County. This "hearing" was for the individual who had run into the bikers from Michigan. A sad case all around....

Lady G and I are scheduling lots of photo shoots for fellow bikers and their steeds. So, let us know if you have a bike you'd be proud to have photos taken of and entered into this here Biker's rag or if you would be willing to model alongside an iron steed or two. Heck, even if you DON'T want them entered into this rag, still, get ahold of us and we'll get you some photos you'll be proud of for your own personal use.

FINALLY, spring has sprung! I've been getting the yard all ready so that when I am at full par, Paradise won't have to kick me in the butt to get me out of the pasture.

On a side note here….to my friends and fellow Loons up North…I hope you all have gotten enough snow because Lady G and I need to get up to Deer Lodge and get ourselves one of those fine pizzas!

For those of you whom haven't been to Deer Lodge, you really do need to stop on in, get a pizza and toss the bull around. No, there really isn't a bull there. It's a: "bring your own bull" kind of place. You know, BOOB. HaHa, I meant to say, BYOB! No, wait, I DID mean to say BOOB!

They are located on Hwy FF, just north of Mercer, WI. (NOT the boobies, DEER LODGE! Wow! Double F??)

Heading North on Hwy 39/51 go north out of Mercer about 2.611432 miles and take a left onto FF. Be careful on this GREAT winding road…you never know who might be heading towards you on YOUR side, just around one of the many blind curves. Also, keep an eye open for pot holes! Here or anywhere else in Wisconsin this year!

While you are up in the area, there are quite a few great roads that you can mosey along on.

All are picturesque and on the types of roads we bikers like. Smooth for the most part, curvy, thru woods and forest and not that heavily traveled. PERFECT!

If you happen to go into Park Falls, there is a real nice, small diner in the middle of town. Stop on in and have a bite to eat or an ice-cream float. Yes, I know this doesn't sound like a bar, but…it ISN'T! One cannot ride on beer and burgers all the time.

While I'm on the kick about getting

out for a ride, please, *please* my friends; be careful out there. I know we all do the safety bit as well as we can, yet, last year was horrendous for bikers in general.

Personally, I lost 2 friends and almost lost another. I'm glad to say, the third friend is doing well and already has her iron steed out on the black ribbon of happiness.

Ok, suffice it to say, this "article" was all over the place but…I'm BACKKKK!

Back in black, I'm about to hit the sack….oh pain reliever….I believe you can get me through the night …Delta Dawn what's that spell you got me on…..roll on down the highway….She's real fine my 409….409…409….. Somewhere on a desert highway She rides a Harley-Davidson……… Roll, roll me away, I'm gonna roll me away tonight Gotta keep rollin, gotta keep ridin', keep searchin' till I find what's right.

Til next month my friends, when the drugs are **completely** out of my system may we see each other out on our 2 wheeled "Chariots of Good Vibrations".

We Just Are….

I hope you all got out on your Iron Horses this past month. Granted, some –ok most- days, we needed rutters and our swimmies. Duckie, EH?

Or, in my case, I'm so wrinkled I was asked to audition for one of the Raisins until I started to sing "I Heard It On the Grapevine". Then…I was just an old, wet, wrinkled man.

Some complained it was too hot last year at this time; now some can complain it's too wet this year. Heck, we're in Wisconsin. Let's be happy we're not battling that 4 letter word! No, not "ex-wife" because that would be a 5 letter word; all dependent upon how you spell it out. No offense to the **ladies** out there. (To those whom are offended, just write my editor. He enjoys getting mail; just don't tell him I told you that).

This past month Lady G and I participated in a couple of rides honoring our veterans: past and present. One down at Hal's Harley Davidson in New Berlin, WI and another at Wisconsin Harley down there in Oconomowoc, WI.

It's always nice to see a group of biker's getting together for a good cause. Keep in mind, lots of motorcycle "clubs" began via veterans.

When some of our veterans came back to the Homeland, it was not that easy to get back into civilian life styles. Since they liked the freedoms of constant moving –and, in some cases- the motorcycles on which they rode for our freedoms, they took the roads closest to what they had become accustomed.

They got together with buddies and fellow vets that they had served with overseas and began a "new" lifestyle here in the states. Be it a hobby or a new way of living, look around you and you'll see what I'm talking about.

Now, back to my story…. Lady G and I joined a couple hundred bikes on each of these rides. Was the weather "perfect"? Not all the time. Yet, when did you ever hear a vet state, "Geez, Uncle Sam, I don't want to protect our freedoms today. It's cold and rainy". NEVER!

Since we live north of these areas, Lady G and I put about 500 miles on the two runs. Yuppers, we put our chaps, leathers, gloves and neoprene masks on.
Glad we did. Brrrrrr!

Both rides were well done. Safety instructions were given before each ride so as all could enjoy and be safe; we had police escorts, etc. to make sure that we could keep moving as a group and we even had food and entertainment. One cannot go wrong with that.

Ride #1: Hal's ride consisted of a great pancake breakfast at his dealership in New Berlin. Keep in mind; this was Hal's 10th Annual Support the Troops Ride and Pancake Breakfast. Keep up the great work Hal!

The local news crew was there to capture this wonderful event for the world to see, or at least the Greater Milwaukee area.

After a safety briefing with our large group of bikers we all rode to the

Harley Davidson Museum in Milwaukee…taking the scenic route.

Once there, the Milwaukee American Legion Band filled the air with great tunes. We enjoyed a presentation done by the Military groups which also included a "laying of the wreath" on the river.

I do need to mention there was a very moving rendition of our National Anthem done by a single military vocalist. We were even witnesses to a heartwrenching "Presentation of Old Glory". (Google this, you will be glad you did).

After the ceremonies, we all dispersed; going to either get something to eat or to take a trip thru the museum. Lady G and I did both.

Ride #2: We met up with a group of bikers at Hogz and Honeez and rode down from Beaver Dam. I must say, it was very nice of the guys there at H-nH as they put on coffee and donuts before we even left the Beaver limits. That kept the morning chill off until we got to Wisconsin Harley in Oconomowoc.

Wisconsin Harley also had donuts and coffee! Plus a variety of other "stomach pleasers".

Why were we all meeting here? Well, this was the "Nation of Patriots Ride".... the fourth year running!

After a nice presentation/speech put on by the dealership and other important speakers, we escorted the flag down to Woodstock, IL. There we presented the flag to the second carrier who will take the flag to the third carrier and so on…. This flag – which left Wisconsin HD on Memorial Weekend- will go thru 48 states and return to Wisconsin HD near Labor Day.

Yes, a true "Nation of Patriots Ride". (Make sure to check with the dealership on the exact date the flag returns).

Down at the dealership in Woodstock, we were treated to entertainment via live band and also had the opportunity to purchase burgers and brats for donations. How could you say no to this?

After all was completed at Woodstock Harley Davidson it was announced that there was a storm moving in. Who'd a thunk, EY?

That meant: Lady G, my sis-in-law Beth -who helped co-ordinate the ride down from Oconomowoc, being a Road Captain in her H.O.G. Chapter- (Rock River H.O.G.), Terry -another member of their chapter- and myself headed north to the Badger.

Since Terry lives near Beer City, he split off at I-43. As for the rest of us, we stayed as a group and went to my brother's and Beth's house to visit my recovering bro from his recent surgery.

David - better known as Digger to quite a few- was glad to see us "po-ta-toe" up to the house. As for Lady G and me, we were glad to see him doing very well!

After visiting for a while, we thought best to get home before rain and darkness blanketed the last leg of our journey.

That night, we put Paradise in her stall.

How could we and hundreds of other bikers do this, put our steeds in their stalls this very night –or any other for that matter?

Well, bikers keep a look out for each other. We point out road hazards, ride as safe as we can and keep our heads together. We are truly one big family.
 So, without further ado, I shall put the final word upon the title of this "rant of words"…**COOL!**

Is that proper English? No.

Is it true? Why not?

Keep it safe my friends!

~Kruser

Campin', Kruser-Style

Well now, isn't this the time of year? We've been waiting for this since last winter… bike-camping time!

Lady G and I got ourselves a brand new, extra-large tent so that I may stand up in it –almost- so as to save me embarrassment from putting my pants on outside of the tent. It's even got a second compartment – the tent- where we can sit in and not get bothered by Wisconsin's state bird, the mosquito!

Granted, we won't use it all too much since we like to mingle with others and see who's in the area. I'm talking about the second compartment, not the whole tent. So, don't fear you won't see my rear!

Even though we camp year in, year out we will be doing a "dry run" to make sure everything we need fits on, in and around the bike. New BIG tent = heavier load. So we must make sure all is well balanced as we know the driver –and sometimes the passenger- is in doubt; one way or another.

One year we left the party a wee bit early and packed the bike up with quite a few other people in our area sitting by their camps. Well, as we kept on a packin', people began to turn their chairs around and watched. You see, we over did it jest a wee bit.

A 3 person tent, cooler, 2 sleeping bags, leathers, rain gear, 2 chairs, usual clothes for the two of us, air mattress and pump, first aid "purse", and a 10' x 10' screen tent later Lady G gets on the bike like she's sitting in a recliner.

Yes, we were a rolling AARP Sporty. Poor Paradise felt like a mule train on that trip….

Will this ever take place again? NO!

It's not safe and it's against:
TYISWKAGAH/SWTYTMMOSRATTT

(Treat your iron steed with kindness and gentleness and he/she will treat you to many moons of safe rides and tales to tell).

So, this year we will be re-doing our thinking and our packing.

As for camping itself? It hasn't changed a bit compared to how we did it when we were
younger…

.

.

.

.

.

.

.

.

.

. ………..

Age 20		Age 50+
Tent on hill with rocks for mattress.		Tent on level ground with air mattress.
When cold and wet out, start camp fire by dipping sticks into gas tank.		When cold and wet out, be nice. Take the little lady to a warm, dry hotel.
When bugs are biting, remove your shirt to show how tough you are. To impress the girls even more, pour a soda down your pants and sit on the ant hills…		When bugs are biting, put an extra shirt on which has been doused with bug repellant. Then spray some more in your hair (or where it used to be), under your arms and on your belly where it's sticking out of that just a wee bit too small

		"Ain't-I-a-Sexy Biker" tshirt.
When darkness falls, feel around without the use of a flashlight. You'll find where you are going, eventually.		When darkness falls, go to bed.
Even if there is no music, sing at the top of your lungs like you're a member of AC/DC.		Put in ear plugs so you don't hear the idiots screaming.
Camp on the outside edge of the campgrounds. This way, you can be first out. Make sure there's a tree tho, just in case you need to do a "leaner".		Camp near the bathrooms but not so close as to have a need for nose plugs. Remember, those plugs are for your ears.

OK, maybe it changed just a tad. Well, at least we 'all still use a tent, right???

Then again, does land whale mean a thing to you?

How-ever you camp keep one thing in mind, there are others around your campsite. Keep it down when it gets to be night time or –preferably- invite them over to partake in some arthritic medicinal/ hot flash remover potions. Alrighty?

'Til next time my friends; keep the wheels rolling.

~Kruser

You Just Might Find…

You can't always get what you want, you can't always get what you want, you can't always get what you want, but if you try sometimes, you just might find, you just might find, you get what you need.

Ah yes…no gettin' stoned now-a-days but I still like the Stones…Rolling Stones for you "young ins" but I am sure you know about Mick Jagger and the gang.

Yup, "You Can't Always Get What You Want" has seemed to hold true for many of us. I remember growing up in a "not-so-rich" household.

My ma did the best she could with what she had and if my brother and/or I wanted something more, well, we learned we damn well better go out and get ourselves a job.

Part time work began at the age of 10 picking weeds, raking leaves and the oh-so-great job of loading a hay wagon AND unloading into the loft for a DOLLAR a wagon. Big bucks indeed! Yet, you did what you needed to "get what you wanted" and sometimes, you just got what you needed.

Well, I've taken that attitude with myself thru out my life and those around me know how much I believe in that. No one gets a free ride…well, except for a few exes –not all exes- but that was out of our hands.

Even Lady G knows what it's like to work for what you want…and to "forfeit" tens of thousands to an ex. You see, no one is immune to working –or doing- what one is supposed to do to earn a good life, a new toy, or a nest egg…except for those darn exes. So, thank you to our court system for making lazy people even lazier. RRRRRRRR

Now, onto something we can all do for ourselves and each other. Biking and events…

This summer has been a very busy one for Lady G and me. We did a lot of landscaping around our homestead and even got the house and garage all painted a new color.

We also went on a lot of bike rides with Paradise, supported quite a few fund raising events, met up with a lot of friends and made a lot of new friends. One thing that stood out to us was the way some of these people acted upon seeing myself there, all be speckled in my chin-skulls.

You see, they would: come on up, shake my hand, ask me if I was the one with the magazine (apparently they couldn't remember the name of this here rag and since my editor's too damn cheap to get me some shirts, well, it's a good thing for my chin-skulls) and then ask me…"Hey, are you going to write about us and what we are doing?"

Well, I am a polite sort of fellow, so I would say, "Well, I am checking it out. You never know what I might write about".

Their reply: "It sure would be nice if you did".

It would then either go to "we're trying to build our business for bikers" or something like "we think this event could really take off, we just need to get the word out there".

Then, they would either talk my ear off or go take care of something else that needed tending. No free t-shirts, no free beer and a burger, no nothing…Yet, they expected something for nothing.

PEOPLE! What the heck do you think I am? A free road for advertising??? I don't think so!

If you need advertising, I can get you hooked up with this really nice editor of a biker rag (THIS ONE) whom I know, and you can PAY for your advertising.

If you really would like me to write about your event, bar, whatever…well then…you damn well better wine and dine me and Lady G because……

You can't always get what you want but if you try sometimes you just might find, you just might find…You get what you need.

We still have some riding left this year, so: Keep it safe my friends!

~Kruser

Hurry Up and Wait?

Sounds like the motto of the truck driver. I've been there, done that!

I just read an article in a cooking magazine which had talked about waiting.

Out in my shop Ozzy's singing about "Life Waits for No One" in his song, "Life Won't Wait".

So, what is it? Do we wait or do we keep moving?

Is it better to get to our destinations as quick as we can or better to enjoy the wait while we can?

I suppose it depends upon the situation.

Driving truck? Well, a lot of getting from one place to another quickly only to find we need to wait for the load to be ready. Now, you can hurry again.

In life, we wait for certain milestones. We wait till we can get our driver's license, turn the legal age to drink, getting married, retiring… Only to find ourselves checking the obits, seeing who's not getting dizzy with us any longer on this blue orb.

Then there's us bikers. Every winter, we wait for riding season to come along so we can get back out on our mighty steeds only to find winter upon us once again…hopefully waiting for spring.

Why "hopefully"? Well, some of us may not make it another riding season. Some of us may be getting just a wee bit "crickety" to get back in the saddle again.

Others may not be with us.

So, what is it? Wait or rush?

I say, "enjoy every minute of it". The waiting isn't all so bad. We just need to use our time more wisely instead of complaining or rushing off to the next place we think we need to be.

We all may not be the type to stop and smell the roses, but one can at least take a breath and exhale.

You don't need to be tokin' or smokin' to breathe in and breathe out. You could be telling a joke with your friends or talking about what you seen as your hair was blowing in the wind. If alone, listen to the birds we don't hear while we are riding our steeds.

Anything!

Life does not need to be rushed thru just to find out we arrived at the end before we truly lived.

Once in a while, all this rushing can cause you to lose a friend because you sped over the gravel of life and your buddy didn't have the skills –or balls- you had and grounded him or herself.

One may not totally lose a friend, but the strings of friendship may be frayed. Only time will tell if those strings of friendship can be re-tied or not. Hmmmm.

Guess we will need to wait.

Whatever you decide to celebrate in the coming holidays, may you -all my friends of the wind- be safe, be warm and join me in waiting for the warmer riding season to return.

As for me and Lady G we will be staying in bed, as we did last year on

Thanksgiving. Getting up to brew a pot of coffee and taking care of Alec-the-Cat. Back to bed to watch the Macy Parade then the Dog Show. Later, we'll get up to get dressed; take Paradise for a ride, then return home to prepare our meal and hold each other….knowing the wait was worth it.

Til next month my friends, take care, stay warm.
Your friend in the wind.

~ Kruser

Frozen Thoughts

As I let my fingers dance across the keyboard of QWERTY, winter's chefs are sprinkling seasoning upon our ribbon of happiness. The turkey remains have been made into soup to slaughter this year's "common cold" and The Muppets Christmas ALBUM plays upon our RECORD PLAYER.

Sounds like I'm into this quarter piece of the Julian calendar, EH? I ask in my faux Canadian dialect.

Well, for the most part, I reply with a resounding NO! But, what am I to do about it?
Partake in a wee bit o' hot chocolate and homemade cookies then hide myself in the shop or in the pages of some bike rag?

Yes, one must make the best of every situation, no matter how gloom it may seem and may be.

As always, I give a lot of thought to my articles –yup, I wouldn't have put money on that one myself. This past week, I had been contemplating upon our brother (sister) hood and where it seems to be heading.

Lady G's and my main get together is with our fellow Loons up in the Northern part of the Badger. We all have a great time and both Gloria and I have made some lifelong friendships these past 3 or 4 years that we've been there. So, that is where I gather my frozen thoughts…

We bikers are getting older, the new comers aren't "blossoming" and the future of the bike gatherings seems to be questionable. It doesn't matter what gathering one is talking about either. Heck, I've been in contact with some people who say they are changing their gathering to golf carts. Another Lady G and I have gone to, well, we just turned right around and left. Looked like a land whale party.

I know we are all aging- some of us not gracefully – and when one pulls into a bike gathering where the bikes are outnumbered by land whales. Nopers, not the "games" I want to see.

Picture this:

Wiener eating contest.

2 shirtless, beer bellied, horn-dogged "men" driving mamas around on golf carts.

They putter over to the wieners hanging from a rope. Yes, ropes as the wieners need to be big enough for the "racers" to see, so…they're sausages on a rope.

Now, the first contestant arrives, mama pulls out her teeth and slaps them onto the sausage. "Got'cha she yelps!" feeling pretty proud of herself.

Next thing she knows, their golf cart hits a bump, out of her tube top pops one of her puppies which bounces off her knee then right into papa knocking him off the cart which he then proceeds to stand up and knocks her teeth from the sausage.

Race couple two, who was only behind by a pee stop, scoots on up, tosses a Viagra onto the sausage, waits for it to "expand" and lets it drop into her lap, yelling at the top of her lungs, "I'm a wiener! I'm a wiener!"

Do we really want to see this happen? I don't believe I can drink that much!

So, what do we do? The youngins seem to have their mind set on what money can buy and what goes with that.

Yes, maybe I'm just an old(er) guy ranting, but let's be honest with ourselves.

Just this past year Papa Loon had a massive heart attack; thankfully he is doing very well. Savage's sister's family lost their home and belongings; taking donations at this time as it took place this past week. Another friend of ours, Kelly broke her leg; thankfully got out on the bike once before the roads disappeared. Friends have been changed or lost to the Heavens of Mother Earth.

So, how do we keep our Biker Family growing? What can we do about it?

Remember, it's more than just the 8-second ride. It's all on how we bring up the little tykes and tykettes.

Pending an answer –or answers- we will do what any good brother and sister should do. We will be by each other's side, helping them in time of need, time of sadness and times of sorrow.

Other times, we will be like any good bro or sis. Together…we'll party like there's no tomorrow! (At least 'til 9pm!)

Until winter relinquishes it's hold upon us, may the warmth of the brother and sisterhood keep us all warm and together. Happy New Year!

Take care my friends! Brrrrrrrrrrrrr

~Kruser

Baby Moons and Memories

Kris...Kris....Kris is the only woman I don't mind giving my money to and yet, she makes me lose my hair?

Yes, that was difficult to get my fingers to extract out of this here keyboard.

Kruser, the man with two ex-wives is paying ANOTHER woman who makes himself lose his hair? Just what does Lady G think of all this? Shouldn't she be the one making this old man lose his hair and take his money????

Well folks, let me say this first: Lady G does NOT take my money. She has her own job, insurance, vehicle, etc. etc. Plus, we are married in spirit and not in "OK folks, when this doesn't work out, Kruser, you give Lady G half of everything you own and half of what you don't own yet" fashion.

Nope, neither "man of the cloth" nor judge was involved. The ring on Lady G's finger? Given to her by yours truly back on Christmas 1981. Yes, 1981…married in spirit.

As for Kris; she's the owner of Guy's and Doll's here in Beaver Dam, WI.

Yes, this tough, old biker –aka Babe Magnet- ok, got carried away with

"Just My Imagination". Where was I going…ah yes, BABE MAGNET! (Nope, better go the other route, the editor would never put that much of "stretch the truth" in his magazine).

Yes, I go to a Hair Salon; now days there aren't many red and white poled Barber shops that one can go to, smoke a stogie and spit in a spittoon. Then get a shave and a cut for a buck.

I've known Kris since 1994. Yes, a long time and many, many hairs ago.

She has seen me –and "styled me"- into many haircuts over the decades. Everything from "Business Man" to "Let's see where this leads".

Heck, she and I even had some very good talks over the years. And laughs? Many, many laughs.

Yes, I consider Kris a good friend, so much so, Lady G and I even stopped over at her house so as the two ladies could meet.

So, anyhooooo… yes, Kris has seen me with hair half-way down my back; held straight down while wet in order to get rid of the Beach Boys wavy style that used to plague me. USED TO!

Today, she has taken me under the clippers to donate to Locks of Love. Yes folks, this makes a total of approximately 3 feet donated on 3 different occasions.

Why at this time of year? Why not wait until spring? Well, this trip to see Kris was my first visit since sometime in 2012 and prospects of my hair doing anything, well, did not look good. Instead, my hair had decided to take "the plunge" and yes, it's entirely my fault.

My grandfather had a very nice head of grey hair and I was hoping to be able to sport the same style when I got older. A fellow co-worker kindly pointed out to me some time ago that, well, "that ain't agoin' to hairpen". (Hairpen? Ha! Old man joke!!)

So why do I blame myself?

To make a long story short, I was taking a shower the other day and started to read my bottle of shampoo's words: "Enriched with 27 vitamins."

I then read Lady G's: "Enriched with 9 vitamins".

Nooooooo!!!!! Say it isn't so!!!!!! I gave my hair an over dose of vitamins!

No wonder as I stood there under the shower head looking at the drain, I could see my hair jump out of their respective places in my head and, with one final Yee Haw begin to follow the trail of those Scrubbing Bubbles!

So that there folks is why I thought I better donate to Locks of Love. It was now or possibly never again. *sniff*

So, as I sit here, my neck freezing in this Winter Blues state that I am in, you may be asking: "Kruser, you had titled this article 'Baby Moons and Memories'. You've gone on and on about the memories of your hair, but where do the baby moons come into this article?"

My reply: "Well, my first car –a 1967 black over red Ford Galaxie- had baby moons. I was pretty proud of those back then.

Today, just walk up behind me and you'll see I am sporting a baby moon where my hair used to be. You know what? I'm pretty proud of that baby moon too!"

Stay safe and stay warm my friends!

~Kruser

Hal's, Bikes and Bears...Oh My!

February 8, 2014. 4 hours of sleep. -8...MINUS! 8 #$@^$&* degrees and, where am I? I'm not in a nice warm bed, cuddled up with Lady G. Oh hell no! I'm sitting in a cold c-c-cold van, under a blanket, my butt being heated up by an electric seat, while Lady G takes us on our first leg of this morning's journey. BRRRRRRRR!

So, what has gotten us up this early, out of our nightly hibernation? Why, the International Motorcycle Show in Chicago, Illinois of course! But still,

BRRRRR! (Less "R's", as the seat is warming me up!)

As I attempt to sneak in a few shut eyes Lady G directs the four wheeled chariot of heat down to Hal's Harley Davidson in New Berlin. (1925 South Moorland Rd, New Berlin, Wisconsin 53151 to be exact; just a few miles from my old work place of the '79-80 time period…Clark Gas Station).

Why Hal's and not directly to the Windy?

We decided to take Hal up on his offer of providing a bus from his place of business –loaded with snacks and drinks- plus entry into the show. What a guy!

OK, not as I figured. This was not just for Lady G and I, the bus was FULL! In reality, we figured it would be, as Hal had a great price for this service. Who couldn't resist?

Due to the weather, we had left as the sun began to yawn resulting in arriving with plenty of time before we took off at 8:30.

The bus trip was great, as we arrived – unscarred- up to the front door for easy entry into the show.

Once in, we all took off in our directions of interest which meant…we scattered! There was an unbelievable amount of "events" taking place inside this one event.

Old bikes, new bikes. Build challenge bikes! Yes, and lots of chrome and other "goodies" to dress up our two-wheeled steeds. Lady G and I also took in a few shows which were put on at the Progressive Stage.

One was on "Long Distance Biking" given by Rick Mayer of Rick Mayer Cycle Seats; another was an info program given by Star Motorcycle School. Both were very informative for all whom attended.
Nicely done!

In between shows, we were entertained by the "School of Rock"; an outstanding group of young musicians! Check them out here: http://chicago.schoolofrock.com .

Heck, at one point we were even entertained by Flo herself, via recorded commercial tho. Darn! (There's nothing like good Flo to go with one's bike. My apologies folks, I was trying an "insurance joke"). OK, back to my article….

Now as far as bike presentation goes, I would have to say that most manufactures of our two wheeled steeds were accounted for: Can-Am to Yamaha and most everyone in between.

For the most part, each manufacturer had something going on for all us attendees. Harley had a demo bike set up where one could practice their shifting while Suzuki had an outstanding, very energetic spokesperson whom got the crowd all wild up over their bikes.

Yuppers, there was something for the youngest attendee to the youngest-at-heart attendee, no one I feel- left disappointed.

During the course of all of this, I had "unknowingly" filled my goodie bag with many souvenirs of this year's show. A wee little something to pass the – hopefully- final days/weeks of this long winter.

Our bus driver, Maurice, was at the ready for when we all re-loaded ourselves into his mighty steed of comfy seats. A professional driver he is too!

Not only was he friendly, but on the way back to Hal's Harley Davidson we passed by 8 accidents due to slippery conditions. Did Maurice fail in keeping us safe? Not one bit; not a slide, nor an abrupt stop did he make. Thank you Maurice!

Once at Hal's Harley Davidson, like cattle we unloaded, shuffling thru the new snow towards our enclosed vehicles.

Was it a good time? Yes.

Was it informative? Again, yes.

All-in-all we were glad we had gone, glad to have taken Hal upon his offer and glad to be back.

We may have the Packer's here in the Badger, but down there in the Windy…Bear Country…they obtained a good amount of money for a couple of burgers and a shared soda.

Beer and cheese anyone?

Til next time my friends! Stay warm. Be safe!

~Kruser

Now's the Time to Think Outside the Box

I drive in a safe manner, for the most part. Doesn't matter if I'm driving 2, 4 or 18 wheels I pride myself on being a fairly good driver.

During the course of my over-the-road I drove a lot of the Eastern Seaboard, down to Peach Land in Georgia on up to the Elk Country of Maine. I also did quite a bit of mid-west and –if I put up a fuss, my dispatcher would get me down to Sweet Tea and Catfish sandwich country.

During the course of those miles I averaged seeing a bad accident at minimum of once a week. Most of those were rear end collisions or making a left turn in front of someone else; need to beat that light, that car, that truck...that bike.

Heck, I had some people who would drive in front of my 80,000 pound ass and put their brakes on until I almost drove over the top of them. Regardless of what you may think, we do not stop on a dime.

There are a lot of sick people out there; those that don't care about others and think life is a video game where you can hit reset and everyone stands back up.

This past month or so I've had people pull in front of me, attempt to pass other vehicles in their lanes coming into my lane creating near head-ons, tail gate me with their high beams and almost been side swiped due to those – most likely- on their phones, etc. etc.

In those instances that I've just mentioned; not only did I have my headlightS on, but I was driving my cage!

So, what do we have here? Potential accidents due to idiots no matter if I was driving with 4 wheels under me or 18 wheels spread out under my belly. I don't believe I need to mention all the times that I had been almost taken out while on two wheels; as I believe you all have been there yourselves.

I just read an article about a motorcycle policeman whom had been killed when a truck had pulled in front of him while he was in pursuit of a speeder. This was in 19THIRTY SIX!!

So, where does this leave us now? What do we do about it? How do we make sure we will survive for the next ride? At the time that I am writing this article, we have already lost a few fellow bikers and that is too many!

I know we are having some "Awareness Rallies" and such, a large one that will be happening in Madison, WI and a lot of smaller ones put on by local bike groups.

What are these "get togethers" doing – or supposed to be doing? They are making the public aware of our presence.

How? By getting together in large groups and holding talks. Others are holding signs that take drivers attention off of where they are going to read signs that in effect say: "Look Out for Bikers". (This last opinion is solely mine and not the editors. Remember the title of this column folks: "Kruser's Point of View").

I would like to make a point on something that we all keep hearing pertaining to this or any other

"Awareness" event motorcyclist stage and that is:
They all try to get others to look out for us bikers.

Good, strong words but I believe they might read better as: "We are looking out for you, please do the same for us". AGAIN, "Kruser's Point of View".

Don't like what I have to say? Then let's meet for a beer and a good burger and we can discuss anything you wish, you're buying.

You see, we cannot depend upon others to keep us safe; we have to do it for ourselves.

Remember when we were growing up? Riding pedal bikes before our beer bellies began to form and our hair hid our eyes? What did our parents tell us? Look out for cars.

Maybe we should begin with that? Then we could follow up with, "Let's all get some more education about riding bikes? Like a beginner or advanced course. (Well worth it).

Maybe something as simple as: Before I get on the bike, I'm only going to have 2 drinks –or maybe none?

Why? Because not only is it my life I'm putting in danger but also my passenger and those around me: bikers, four wheelers and pedestrians???

How about this one? Before I go on the road, I'm going to make sure my bike is safe. Tires, controls, brakes, etc.

We need to take responsibility for ourselves because we are the only ones we can depend upon.

What can we do to help ourselves live to see another day; without having to be forced into wearing dome lids or nuclear glowing vests?

The answer which would avoid most of these deaths:

Common sense, education and looking out for others; from both bikers and cages.

Let's think outside the box before the lid closes; leaving our loved ones behind, wondering: "If only ---------".

Keep it safe my friends!

~Kruser

War

War....it never stops killing. Long after the ones whom were the reason for its initialization are long gone.... line after line, brother after brother, sister after sister... still dying; decades after the "treaty of peace" has been signed.

"Kruser, coming into work tomorrow"? Yes, I replied to Huck's question; followed by, "You?"

"No, going over to visit some friends; Jim and Judy. I think you know Jim. He had his stomach replaced, cancer ridden, doing ok; at least he's hanging in there. Third one I know whom had this done since the war began".

"Ya, I know Jim. Tell him I say Hi and to keep fighting. It'll be good to see him out this summer riding that bike of his. Wish his wife enjoyed it, but glad she doesn't mind when he comes along with us 'GOLD Ol' Boys'".

"Sure, I'll tell him. Yes, she's a good woman. Part of me thinks she's glad to get rid of him those few times we take off for a couple of days…gives her a break".

We both smiled.

"Yes, Jim's got a warped sense of humor, he does, he does". We started to break into a laugh as we each began to recall some fun times on the road with Jim.

Huck headed his way; I mine, as we needed to finish up our tasks before the shift ended.

I believe we both knew –as did Jim that this visit tomorrow may be the last time Huck and Jim would see each other. Usually after our friends had their stomachs replaced, as much as the doctors tried, their skills were not enough for the human body to accept the replacement part.

Each of our friends had gone into battle, to protect these great United States of ours. Many sacrificing family needs to protect all of us on the home front.

I will always kick myself in the ass for never joining the service. I had tried three times. First at 16 but my ma wouldn't allow me. Next when I was 20, then I cracked up a bike and wrecked my knee. Third – thinking they'll let me in now, my knee was healed; but the "woman" I was with didn't want that, so I stayed behind. Bad move on my part, battle would've been easier.

Do I believe in war?

Let me answer that as the biker I am. I believe in taking care of things that need to be taken care of in a timely matter. Yes, some things require more thought, more planning. No doubt.

Yet, in this day and age; with all our knowledge and skills why does it take so long to take care of what "we" deem as a potential threat? Can we not determine the source, zero in and take care of the "target"?

Why does it take so long?

No, I am not educated in this area so I cannot answer these questions in an educated fashion. Yet, I believe many of us have those same questions, those same concerns for all of our loved ones who protect us from harm.

Is it the politician's way or the military way?

I do not know for sure. Neither am I here to give that answer, only to leave you decide your conclusions based upon what you know, what you believe.

Do I stand behind our soldier's when they are fighting for our protection? Damn right I do!

Do I stand behind our soldiers when they come home?

Again, damn right I do! If needed, I will stand in front of them to take a bullet from some idiot whom blames the war, police action, conflict upon these fine men and women. Why?

Because that's who us bikers are, the "take no shit" breed. Doesn't matter if I believe the reason for the presence of our military, I will always stand behind them. Remember, they are carrying out orders, put out by politicians in suits, in offices.

War....it never stops killing. Long after the ones whom were the reason for its initialization are long gone.... line after line, brother after brother, sister after sister... still dying; decades after the "treaty of peace" has been signed.

Now, did the above really take place?

Was it reality or a dream I awoke from at 4:35 in the morning and sat down at my keyboard to get these words out before transitioning into Edgar Allen Poe, helplessly hearing the heartbeat of a long passed on friend? Or is it a premonition of losing another one of my brothers or sisters?

To those I will never meet and to those I work with, party with, ride with whom have served: "Thank you!"

My friends, as we enter a new riding season, please stay safe; I'd like to hear you complain this winter again. Have fun now!

~ Kruser

Fellow riders, please keep in mind the Nation of Patriots ride this year which is May 24, 2014. This will begin at Badger Harley-Davidson over in Madison, WI.

Ceremony begins at 11am with kickstands up at 12pm. At that time the group will be headed for Woodstock HarleyDavidson, Woodstock, IL. Great time, great cause!

Black and White

hat does that mean to anyone?

Lots of things I suppose? It could be: The keys to a piano, a zebra, or possibly even Halle Berry?

To me, it means a simpler time; a time before stress became a part of life, a time before I ever thought of meeting Halle, a time before my ma got us a color TV.

I was just a youngin' back then, circa 1970.

My day consisted of riding my bicycle for miles and miles, running and discovering stuff in the Kettle Moraine and watching cartoons where they hit each other over the head with clubs or tried to blow up road runners.

Yes, a simpler time.

Fast forward to 2014. Summer's finally here and Lady G and I have the key to Paradise, which means we can go back to the black and white days of yesteryear; without the pedaling.

We can bike the whole day and de-stress while taking the back roads. Enjoying the sights and sounds away from daily living, cluster $%^&)@ roads and responsibilities.

Today we ride, we de-stress; we take roads near and far from us that we rarely get to enjoy.

Our day began by getting up at the crack of 10am, after the cock has tired himself out at the crack of dawn. No doodle-doodle here, we like to "read" late into the night.

We started out with a slow easy ride of about a mile or so to partake in the local ABATE brat fry, talked with a few fellow members and had dinner.

We then put on another whopping mile to surrender next months' paycheck to a local business. The joys of home ownership amaze me! More money than I was quoted over the phone, so much more that they should've had their business on the corner; but, in all honesty, they do a great job.

Finally, we get back in the saddle and point Paradise in the direction we are heading: Keyeser, WI.

We had heard of a place called "Gilbertson's Store" where it seemed time had stood still -a store/bar combination- and that the owner always had something for female "Keyeser Virgins". This should prove interesting.

The community is farm based, which in itself is hard to find now-a-days. So, back roads are where we are opening the reins on Paradise.

We meandered along the country county roads leading to our destination and getting detoured for construction which took us over another nice road. No problem with that today.

Enjoying the scenery, warm air and sunshine that was the weather of the day -Hey, I could be an after-the-fact weatherman, EH? Any whooo…. we forgot about stress.

Parched from the Midwest sun and full of anticipation, we arrived at our treks end. Tying Paradise up to a nonexistent hitching post, we beat the journey's dust off our jeans and meandered into "Gilbertson's Store".

We were greeted by how I remember Sherman's store in Eagle as being, only slightly smaller in size. Yet, amazing in -and of- itself, simply in the way it presented it's innards to us.

Our eyes were witnessing "The Days of Yesteryear" where items to be purchased were neatly placed upon shelves; some of which only the store-keep could get for the customer.

There were cleaning supplies to cigars; paper towels to canned goods. Looking into the bowels of the establishment, towards the back of the business was bar stools and a few tables.

So, what to do now? Well, mosey on down, throw a leg over a stool and order a couple of cold ones to get rid of the dust in our teeth and the sore in our saddles.

Down at "the bar" we were greeted by a few town folk and Kenny the proprietor. A friendly group indeed!

One of the guys there talked with me about how he had some fast bikes and wanted to take a look at Paradise.

While we did so, Kenny and Lady G visited and had some good, hearty laughs.

Upon my return, Lady G and I were told some of the history in this family business and how it all began, a tale of the hundred-year anniversary and a few other interesting items which I will not divulge here. Ask Kenny when you stop in, he'll be glad to share his knowledge of the "Black and White Days".

After taking a few photos inside and out, it was time to bid our new friends a farewell, a see you later, and to get back out on the trail.

As we straddled Paradise, she reared her handle bars and with a mighty "Hi-o-Paradise" we galloped on to new roads, new adventures, and new friends.

Oh, you're wondering what Kenny had for Lady G? Well, let's just say, she's not a "Keyeser Virgin" no more.

Ah yes, black and white. It doesn't get much better than that.

Keep it safe my friends!

~Kruser

"Lady G and Kenny"

My Brother's Keeper?

I took my cage just today to a nearby town as a fellow brother had some wheels he wished to have me work on for him.

Since I'm such a nice fellow, I told him I could pick them up and save him the trip; me being in his town for a dentist appointment anyway.

On my way back to my home-20 I had a "biker" come off a side street and hang onto my left, rear bumper. He continued to do so as we hit speeds upwards to 60 mph.

Since I am a biker myself, I made a move to allow him to pass when it was safe. As luck would have it, I would meet him at the stop sign. Again, being such a nice fellow, I drove along side of him to give him the following advice: "Not all of us are bikers. Those whom aren't could've done you in back there".

His reply: "I do this all the time. It's all good".

I'm not sure if he recognized me behind the wheel, but I know who he was. He's a well-known "biker" in the area and a real nice guy. I've helped him out in the past when he was in need and would do so in the future.

Just a couple of days prior to this, a "flock" of four of my Southern friends were nearly run into by a cage passing on the shoulder.

Again, as luck would have it, they met him at the traffic light.

To keep a long story short, their words were, "Usually we have our gun…" So, what does this mean? You would've taken their life?

Where would you be sitting today had you done that? Just cause for shooting them down? No!

Do I understand why you're pissed off in this instance? Damn right I do! Yet, you can NOT shoot when YOU deem it to be so. Think!!!

A couple of weeks prior to this, a friend of mine was telling us how he got his bike "more power".

Then he proceeded to tell us he only got up to 90 mph –on a 65 mph road- before his wife slapped him alongside the head.

Come on now, you are closer to death than you have life left at this point in your ages, don't rush the end result of living. Why do you need to go faster on a public road?

You are only as tough as long as your hide lasts on the pavement when you go down. That isn't long; but don't worry, you'll probably not even know what hit you...or what you hit.

What do all the "happenings" above have in common? Stupidity!

I'm not saying I have never done these things, but as I get older, well, because I have stopped doing a lot of these things, I am becoming wiser.

I have a fellow biker brother whom has a patch upon his vest which reads: "I am my brother's keeper".

What does this mean? The answer is that we help one another out when: life gets a bit tough *or* we do something stupid.

We are there for you. Problem is if you don't listen there isn't much we can do except let you go on your own path and hope you don't take someone else with you.

The first individual would leave a child behind, the "flock" of four would leave numerous children and grandchildren behind and the last individual, well, he would've taken his wife with him but left children behind.

Doesn't matter if these kids are infants or grownups either, they would still be left behind.

As for "I am my brother's keeper", that just may turn into "I was my brother's pallbearer".

Now, how would you like your "Remembrance Patch" to be designed?

To those whom know what I am talking about, may you be healthy in your older age. To those whom do not understand, well, you're just in this "biking" for the "bling clothing" and an early casket.

Try to keep it safe my friends!

(Even though we should always keep safety in mind, enough is enough; next month begins new subjects, more "kinder" topics. The "herd" will thin itself out…) ~Kruser

IMAGES

Crickets and Cat Man-doo-doo, that last column of mine got some responses, even one from a TV show pertaining to bikers. That's good to hear; at least I know some of you read my column. Better than that, some of what I say is getting a few of you to think; while other columns are just "nice to read". Thank you!

Now, I did have a mellower topic for this month, but decided maybe we could put some closure on last month's article. So, with that I present to you this month's topic, "IMAGES".

Let's start with a nice table set for two…opposites I suppose you could say, on the "biking scale":

Rides a Gold Wing	Rides a Harley
Holds a full time job	Lives off family, friends and the state
Loves to cook for his family	Can't even take care of himself
Participates on rides to raise money for others	Rides bar-to-bar bragging to anyone that'll listen to how much better he is than others

"So, Kruser", some of you might be asking, "What the hell are you saying? You just put down every single Harley rider and we're about to kick your ass in."

Now hold on Hog-a-Roos that table -as small a table as it is- lists some of the stuff the general public sees certain bikers as being...you know "stereo typing". Similar to crotch rockets being death missiles (which is only the case if the rider is an idiot) and trikes are for "old" people.

This is what happens when the un-educated population sees a biker; or anyone else/thing they do not understand nor like. They stereo-type everyone into one group as it makes it easier on themselves when they start their finger pointing.

They do not take the time, nor want to take the time, to really look at the problem. That is where we come in as a group of bikers.

It doesn't matter what we may ride: Gold Wing (I've owned 3 myself), Crotch Rockets, those damn loud Harleys (insert SMILE), or a classic Indian (insert ENVY), Yamaha, Suzuki, or Kawasaki.

We need to give a better IMAGE of whom we are when we are near the general population; and when it comes to safety, that goes without saying….EVERYWHERE!

Now, let's add some more to that table. Oh, and my apologies, I had the Gold Wing and Harley rider **mixed up**. Now, for your viewing pleasure, "The Table":

Rides a Harley	Rides a Gold Wing
Holds a full time job	Lives off family, friends and the state
Loves to cook for his family	Can't even take care of himself
Participates on rides toraise money for others	Rides bar-to-bar bragging to anyone that'll listen to how much better he is than others

Works with those around him	Controls those around him
Goes to church/prays for themselves and others	Goes to church/asks for himself
Long Hair	Short Hair
Beard	No beard
Jeans and t-shirt	Dresses like he drives a green tractor
Is a member of a motorcycle "club"	Does not get along with others

So, how did that make you feel, switching the two riders around? Not good? Good!

This is what happens when we all start saying, "Well, who cares? They aren't talking about me."

Yet, we are all in this together.

We...are...motorcyclists.

Some of us are more "biker" than others. Still, one in the same in the respect of what we ride; two wheels, sometimes three.

Keep in mind my friends; the info on the tables is only an example. Not all Harley or Gold Wing riders are as the above tables depict, yet this is what happens when people "generalize".

Not only do some of them "generalize" but some of them would have had the

Harley Rider as "the parasite". We, being the motorcyclists, know that it doesn't matter what bike you ride, *anyone* can be a "parasite".

Each of us is different in our own ways, yet we should all work together toward the common goal of allowing all motorcyclists to look good in the general public's eye.

Heck, for example Lady G and myself – although partial to the mean green machines of JD will still ride with those whom like, oh, I don't know, let's say the "red" tractors.

We as a group of MOTORCYCLISTS need to present an image in which it does not give the general public ammo to shoot us down, but of one where we are responsible for ourselves and those around us.

No brown nosing needed, only decency. If not, prepare to don your suit of armor and get your asses rusted to your trusty steeds. (Yes, I know it's impossible to rust your asses to leather seats, but if you envision a hot biker woman sitting on the gas tank facing you, arching her back over the handle bars, glistening in the sun from all the sweat beading out of the seams of her 2 piece armored suit, well, something, somewhere is going to rust).

Remember; let us ALL be part of the solution, not part of the problem.

Keep it safe my friends! ~Kruser

Sprocket Connection

Fall is upon us and I'm staring at a blank page, thinkin' it may be sooner than later that I'll need to put Paradise in her stall to wait out the upcoming winter months. Why so darn soon?

Well, I may have broken my clutch hand and in order to keep the swelling from getting "out of hand" –yes even in pain I jest- I had to take myself off the bike last week. Simply put I wasn't safe.

It took place about two weeks ago, when Lady G and I moved the little "Kitten" into her new room at college.

After all these years of moving her in and out of college, this year we forgot a hammer to adjust her bed. Get this, my hand is not "the hammer" it once was. Go figure.

Yes, things change over time. Our memories forget what really was but remember what we think they "was".

Old Thunder and Lightning, those two arms of mine still rumble at times, but they aren't the storm they once were. Yet, they take care of things the best they can.

No different than anything else you could say. Us, our bikes or our friendships…they all get old and need "maintenance".

Friendship you say Kruser? That is a strange one, where the heck are you going with this? I mean, I can see us getting old or our bikes "nostalgic" but friendships?

Remember when we were young and rode our pedal bikes year round, going to friends' houses, down to the old swimming hole or the new tree house?

Back when most of us were thinner and had more hair?

What were we doing without realizing it? Maintaining our friendships.

Now that we are older and have motorized bikes, what are we doing? We are maintaining our friendships and possibly saving –or at least extending- our marriages for another day.

Even tho the times have changed, biking still keeps us together. The trips may not be as long, but oh, the stories we tell about them keep us close together.

The trips of today might be day trips instead of week-long adven- tures due to health or responsibilities to family and work, but we still take those road trips together.

Thru these road trips, poker runs and week end camp outs the biking community has some of the tightest bonds of friendships. We're there for one another, brother and sister.

As we get older we start to become the –hold back the laughter now- we start to become the "wise old owls" for the young ones joining our flocks.

Next time you're at work, look around you. How many true friendships do you see? Now, recall the last biker get together you were at, how many true friendships did you see there? Even co-workers at a bike gathering have a true friendship …we have a bond.

As our hair changes color or the breeze blows some strands off; as we put on the extra layer to keep our liver spots warm and our varicose veins flowing, may we welcome this coming fall with open arms for our friends, recalling the past year of rides…and planning new ones for next year.

My friends, may you be warm and safe as we travel thru this season of the calendar and of our lives.

~Kruser

Ancestral Ride

After a month of waiting for Thunder (my left fist) to heal, I wasn't going to waste anytime sitting around if it wasn't on Paradise.

The weather was changing into a nice fall temperature, even more toward a real nice spring temp. It was time to ride!

I had gone on a ride with a buddy on the previous Friday; we "obtained" 157 miles of great roads under our steeds that day.   Sunday found Lady G able to go along on what started as a 25-mile ride; turning into a 156 mile fun-filled day.

Monday, well, Monday was a "me" day.

It had been quite some time since I had said to Paradise, "Hey buddy, it's time to get some dust in our filter, just you and me".

Years ago -pre-Lady G- there would be plenty of "me" rides, as the women I'd been with had simply stepped upon my last nerve and strangled the poor thing until it became "Smurfy-blue" with a hint of Charlotte's tattered web spelling out "kill me, killlll meeeee". Thankfully, those days are in the past.

So, Monday morning, bright and early, Lady G goes off to work. As for myself, I drag my old frame out of bed at the un-known to any sane man of 9am. Arghhhh!

After some coffee and small talk with Alec-the-Cat, I head out to the stable to see if Paradise is awake. Yuppers, she's so excited, she is pooping a wheelie and spinning her back half in circles. That's my girl.

I had done a pre-ride check of her the night before so with the go-go juice in me, we were both ready to conquer a trip I had planned on doing for many a year. Cemetery ride!

WTF Kruser?!?! Cemetery ride? Let me explain my fellow tuning forks.

First off, "Tuning fork" explanation: We are riding our steeds, sitting upright, both arms out on the reins while the road bumps and rumble strips make us vibrate.

Before you "Wing Riders" say you don't vibrate, that is not necessarily true. You're just a wee bit "flat" compared to us Hog riders whom are more "sharp". Yes, I can say that as I've ridden Wings since 1984.

"Cemetery ride" explanation: A ride to multiple cemetery destinations to visit those whom had gone before us. In my case, having traced my family tree back between 200 and 230 years, dependent upon which branch we are talking about, I was going to visit relatives. Now, onward…

Paradise and I left our farmette in route to Waukesha, WI. A beautiful, warm, sunny morning indeed. We did not want to take any big roads, so we followed Hwy 67 south towards Oconomowoc enjoying the view of a few trees that had changed color.

Yup, a few yellows and many shades of browns were witnessed this day; of course, lots of greens were being reluctant. It was looking like another "usual" fall, not like the ones I remembered as a kid growing up in the Southern Kettle Moraine.

I had heard about a bar in Monterey –a spot off Hwy 67, north of Oconomowoc that I should try out sometime- so Paradise and I pulled off and took the road straight to the drinking hole.

Fairly busy, but then again it was noon and I was sure people were enjoying a good bar burger. Mmmm. I was wro- wr-w-…in error.

Once inside I was mortified to find out they only served some type of food that resembled a flying saucer. Don't know about you, but I'm not too keen upon them thar discs when I am looking forward to a good burger.

All of that aside, the establishment reminded me of a good ol' time bar, the people were friendly, and the bar tender was nice. As busy as she was, she still took time to talk with all the patrons and made sure their drinks were full. Speaking of which...do NOT order the English "Craft" beer. (OK, you can, but I'm warning you...if it smells like piss, tastes like piss, it's English beer. Apparently, it IS a long boat ride across the pond. Yuck!)

After rinsing my mouth out, it was back onto Paradise with a giddy-up go.

We took Hwy 67 south to East 18 which turned out to be a good decision. Sure it's a somewhat busy road, but quite scenic. It's also got a pull off by a bridge where one can do a little fishing or leave behind some English-WHAT-THE-HELL-WAS-THAT beer.

On the way back from the new "English Channel" I also seen some different mushrooms, or is it a side effect that's still lingering? Nope, real live mushrooms! These didn't talk to me.

I proceeded into Waukesha, stopped off where my sister Cat works and visited for a wee bit as it had been almost a year since we had seen each other. Where does that time go?

Now, Talley-ho! (Oh no!) For the first cemetery: Prairie Home. This is where my great-great and great grandparents are buried. Not only that, but Les Paul is also buried here.

I stopped in the office and talked to a lovely lady whom directed me to Les' final resting area and proceeded to allow Paradise to take me there; not far from my ancestor's area. As Paradise took a rest, I walked over by Les.

Amazing the layout! Also, the guitar picks that were left behind; it makes you wonder who all have stopped by to say "Thank you for all you've done for music". He had made many a great career.

After visiting everyone, I gathered up the reins once again…and then got out of the saddle. Darn, it sure is getting a bit cool. I put on my long-sleeved t-shirt and proceeded to the next stop; the Presbyterian Cemetery in Vernon.

As I rolled up to the stop light at Sunset Blvd. I heard something behind me and, looking in my mirrors, it looked like a dust storm blowing across the road. This isn't good. Dust or rain it didn't matter as long as it stayed behind me. I got fortunate.

Taking Hwy 164 to Vernon, the temps began falling and the sky got "ugly". What happened to the sun and warmth? Rrrrrrr

I stopped only for a short time to tell Grandma and Grandpa I missed them along with my Aunt and Uncle. (Grandma is one reason I "can" food as much as I do). Then it was time to get back on the road towards Big Bend; I had no idea how much this weather was going to change.

At Big Bend I took a little bit more time as there were a few more relatives here. The special one to me being Grace and her husband. I used to take my daughters down to visit and have coffee cake and coffee while we chatted at the kitchen table. Because of those times, Lady G and I try to keep that "formality" going when we have company.

Looking towards the north, well, it wasn't looking good in that direction at all. Darkness was rolling in and it looked like rain; the jacket went on this time.

I did take County X back towards Hwy 83, going thru the Vernon Marsh. Beautiful, curvy roads. I mean, if it's going to rain it's going to rain. I might as well enjoy the ride.

The intent was to get home via Hwy 60, but I decided to hook onto Hwy 67 instead. A wee bit fewer miles since the clouds looked like they were about to sob uncontrollably.

Stopping off to feed Paradise, I put on the clear goggles and gloves; I knew we were going to finish this beautiful day totally opposite of how it began.

Leaving the petrol station –damn English beer is still with me- PETROL station?!?!?! Either way, a few miles later I felt as if I were inside the book of: "Winnie-the-Pooh and the Blustery Day".

Yes, the last 40 miles ol' Paradise and I got pelted with strong winds and frigid water bullets. What could be worse? Oh crap, is that hail? No. Good. Keep riding Kruser.

As Paradise and I rolled into her stall, I turned the furnace on and took in the heat. KIZZ came in with "Hotter than Hell" over the stereo, but I knew that was bull. Not here at least. Still, we were out of the rain and had a great ride; even if the temp went from a dry, sunny 74 degrees to a wet and windy 52 degrees.

What did we get out of this day? A day of me and my mighty steed, cleared thoughts in the head and a ride I had planned on taking for many years but never had the time.

Down the road, when I tell people this story around the warmth of a camp fire, you probably realize the story will change a bit; that the rain was coming down in tubs and the wind blew out the sun, right?

My friends, may you all stay safe and warm!

~Kruser

Thank you!

In just a few short, dark, c-c-cold weeks another year will have gone by. As most of you, I also will be asking myself, "where had it all gone?"

Some of us will reminisce about our trips that we had taken, get-togethers with old friends and trips in which we made new ones.

Still some of us may be healing either from a mishap in our two-wheeled world or other area of life while some of us may be mourning over the loss of a fellow brother or sister. Time does not wait for us, so we must use it wisely while we still have our second-hand spinning in circles.

As for me, the year had been full of surprises; good and bad, some of which you may be reading about next year. I also hope some of you may be reading my new book which should be out by the time you hold this in your hand. If you wish more info on that, please email me.

Lady G and I realize Veterans Day and Thanksgiving have passed, Christmas is nearer as is New Year's.

Many, many reminders during this time of year where we should remember those around us- known and unknown by name to us- to be thankful for all we have because of what we do for ourselves and those around us whom help us get there.

These past two years of writing for all of you, making jokes along the way and sometimes putting a boot up someone's ass, well these are words I believe need to be spoken at times. We need an eye opener every now and then, but we also need to keep the words enlightened at times too.

Yet, without all of you whom take the time out of your lives to read the words I tickle out of old "QWERTY", my column would be in vain; no one to smile at a stupid remark or get pissed off at a serious one in which they may see themselves.

Your comments, suggestions and attitudes –good and bad- have been, and always will be, appreciated!

The time you spent reading this column Lady G and I cannot return, all we can say is "Thank you!" for reading "Kruser's Point of View".

May you all have a warm, safe winter and a very Merry Christmas!

~ Kruser

Lady G and Her Big "O"

I recall a time in my mid-30's when I began to worry about what is going to happen when I get older. Am I going to be able to get it up anymore or not?

Now, here at the age of 53 it seems that I just can't get it down. Yes, it does make Lady G happy, to say the least.

She is getting the big "O" in ways she was not expecting at all. Well, maybe that quite isn't correct to say, let's call it the "little O". Yet, there is one heck of a smile upon her face.

I can just hear some of you out there now…Harold's reading my column when all of a sudden his jaw drops open with an "Oh My Gosh Ethel! Come on in here!"

Kruser is talking about giving Lady G the Big O!"

Ethel replies: "Oh Harold, you old fool, what the tarnation are you talking about?"

"It's right here on this page right in front of me glasses! I can't believe he's writing about this and you won't even let me do you in the a…"

"Shut up Harold and let me see that article that nice Kruser feller has written this time! Geesh!"

Well, before Ethel and Harold end up with heart attacks, let me straighten out the words for the rest of you. I am talking about camping.

"Oh, now what in tarnation? That poor feller has done near lost it Harold!!!"

Now, now Ethel, let me explain. I had written a past column some time ago talking about when I was a youngin' and there was a time we would throw the tent up and sleep on the ground on the incline of a hill.

Now that I have gotten to this age, the getting it down is pertaining to getting on my knees and crawling into the tent, mornings being pure "electrifying" as every nerve still alive within this old container let me know they still exist.

No, I have not gone true "land whale" but I have gone the route of purchasing a pop-up camper to pull behind Olympus; our 2011 Electra Glide. This is where the "little "o"" comes in; Ollie as we call him.

A few years back we had been at a biker get together when we noticed a couple of bikers pulling into the camping area with campers in tow.

Lady G and I watched in fascination as they assembled these "rooms of paradise" in less than 10 minutes while sipping a gallon of moonshine. Quite impressed we were, as we moseyed on over and introduced ourselves.

We made some new friends that weekend, shared some moonshine, some stories and some belching, along with some nasty headaches the next morn. (Yes, Lady G and I were about 5 or 6 years younger, so we were still "over" enjoying a few. I'm just glad we still remember those times.)

I recall mentioning to Guy –owner of one of the campers- that one day I hope to get one of those campers.

That one day became this past December.

I got ahold of Trailermaster out of Illinois, talked with a Peggy and emailed her our "wants" and our needs".

A few weeks later, it was in our driveway and I was speechless!

You see, I did not pick this up myself, but yours and my most liked editor of this here biker rag, Dan, had done me the favor of bringing the camper up to our place.

He even brought it up in an enclosed trailer!

Yes, Dan had seen the camper before me or Lady G and his words when we unloaded it in my driveway?

"Before we unload this, if you want, I can take it home with me". He was quite impressed with the camper himself!

This camper contains a king-sized bed, a cooler rack on the tongue, swivel hitch, lighting, 6' x 6' front room, windows/screens, 25 cubic feet of storage. Oh heck, there is so much to this, you really need to take a look at their site yourself.

www.trailmasterinc.com – Tell them Kruser sent you.

So, as I was saying, I can't get it down anymore, but I sure can bring it up as much as Lady G wants me to and then some. Heck, once it's up it can stay up for days, maybe even weeks! But, again, we are talking about campers here.

Oh, yes, I know I had titled this Lady G and her BIG "O", but I can't tell you about that in this here PG magazine.

That's between Lady G and me. Just keep in mind; if you see Olympus and Ollie anywhere, if Ollie is bouncing, well, you know what comes after Kru…I mean the letter "N".

Keep it warm and safe my friends! Riding time is one day closer!

~Kruser

Halle and Me

Man what a crazy night! I had a dream it was Feb. 2015 and we were having a snow "storm" with winds up to 30 mph. Yet, I awoke this morning, and all was calm. Calm and peaceful! Why? IT WAS SUMMER!

Yes, my time of year and today was an extra special day because I was going

to go on a ride with a very good friend of mine, Halle B.

Yes, that is correct, Lady G told me I had to go and get away from the house and finish writing my new book. She even said it was ok if Halle came along!

Now, that is trust! And, willpower on my part…or maybe Halle's?

Either way, it was going to be a great time. We were going to go up to the campgrounds for a few days, get away from the "chores of home", ride, write, write and write some more.

For a couple of days there would be no TV, radio, or people. Yes, this would be great; just me, Halle and Paradise.

I got the bike packed up the night before and strapped Halle onto the back seat area so she wouldn't fall out.

She did put up a bit of a fuss saying her hair would get mussed, but I told her it was going to get "mussed" later anyway…from the ride…on the bike…to the campgrounds! Geez people. (hehe)

We left early in the morning, after Lady G had taken some photos of us for

memories sake and with a kiss to Lady G, Halle and I rode Paradise off into the high noon sun. (OK, maybe not, because we would've had to go straight up then. Not a good thing unless you're on a rocket).

It was a nice riding day until we got to Princeton. That's where Halle decided she had enough with the riding and attempted to get off the bike.

I heard her "pages" flapping in the wind and with my right hand, reached back and grabbed ahold of her before she hit the pavement.

"My gosh woman!" I thought to myself as I pulled over to the side of the street. RRRRRRRRRRRRRRRR!

Not wanting to cause a scene, I simply took Halle and strapped her in under her bungee cords and told her to be a good woman that we would get to the campgrounds before she realized. She just gave me a cold stare. Almost like she wasn't even there!

Back on the road to our destination I thought things would go better. Yup, I was wrong.

Halle started to loosen things up such as the sleeping bag and other needed items! That darn woman, you would swear she didn't want to be with me! Pulling over into a parking lot, I had a little talk with her and I must say, she was speechless! Not a single word came out of her mouth as I repacked Paradise!

Poor Paradise, with everything we had to pack for Halle, Paradise looked like a pack mule on this trip.

Back on the road and a few hours later, we three arrived at our destination. Finally!

Unsurprisingly, Halle wasn't much help in the unpacking of Paradise, much less putting up our tent or screen tent either.

Heck, I even had to drag the picnic table into the screen tent by myself! Geez, how did she think I was going to do my writing without the table inside to keep the insects away? Selfish!

Apparently she thought this trip was all about her! Nope! No way, no how, noooooo…

Turns out she was fairly correct as she was adamant about me serving her breakfast of coffee and pop tarts; making sure she was not in the sun for too long and also that she got to sleep in the tent while I slept in the screen tent on top of the picnic table, using my leather jacket as a blanket. Yup, reminded me of the old days!

I remember that night I slept under the stars inside the screen tent. It was an awfully hot night, but with Halle snoring as she had, she inhaled the Arctic cold front which kept me cool. That was nice of her, or so I thought!

That morning I awoke to such a scream of my own as when I opened my eyes I was staring into a foot of white, powdery, COLD s%#%...I mean SNOW!

Oh geez! Lady G is not going to be so understanding of my doings of this night I thought over a shiver!

It turned out that it was indeed February 2015...approximately 1am in the morning....37 beers under my belt...and I had passed out on the way to the outdoor p-room after the Superbowl had gotten done, A FEW HOURS AGO!

Oh, how I dislike winter!

Stay warm my friends, every day is one day closer to riding time!
~Kruser

Final Thoughts

My friends, I hope you have enjoyed these stories. I also hope it has brought you some laughs and maybe made a friend or two around the campfire discussing them with each other.

Some of these stories were "different" while others were very serious; that is where the great conversations happen.

Others may have brought out an emotion or two; either way, I hope you have enjoyed yourself within these pages.

Please take a look at my website: www.AlecGould.com for my other books; along with my schedule for book signings/events.

I cover a wide range of styles from the style you have just read to Edgar Allan Poe style.

Stay safe my friends! May we meet on the road someday…

~Kruser

www.ingramcontent.com/pod-product-compliance
Lightning Source LLC
Chambersburg PA
CBHW050631300426
44112CB00012B/1751